MW01076657

TO KURTIS AND ALISA

with love.

Julie

Feb 17, 2012

ALSO BY JULIE BERGMAN

Los Angeles Fires of the Heart (book of poetry)
Custom Guitars, A Complete Guide to Contemporary Handcrafted Guitars
(contributing Author)

THE FINDER

Poems of a Private Investigator

Julie Bergman

Illustrated by Hans Diebschlag
Introduction by Nancy Wilson

Undercover Books

Copyright © 2011 by Julie A. Bergman
Illustrations Copyright © 2011 by Hans Diebschlag

All rights reserved. No part of this book may be
reproduced or transmitted in any form or by any means,
graphic, electronic or mechanical, including photocopying,
recording, taping or by any information storage and retrieval
system without permission in writing from the publisher,
except for the inclusion of brief quotations embodied in critical
articles and reviews.

ISBN 978-0-9644458-0-2

Pacing the Cage
Written by Bruce Cockburn
© 1996 Golden Mountain Music Corp.
Reprinted by permission.

Lyric by Heart from "Wheels," Published by Universal Music Publishing,
© 2010 Heart General Partnership. Reprinted by permission.

Illustrations: Hans Diebschlag

Book Design: Isaac Hernández/IsaacArt.com

Undercover Books
PO Box 1157
Topanga, CA 90290

Library of Congress Control Number 2011944810

Manufactured in the United States of America
First Printing: January 2012

For Nancy Wilson and Hans Diebschlag,
soulmates and muses who rocked this work to life.

Sometimes the best map will not guide you
You can't see what's around the bend
Sometimes the road leads through dark places
Sometimes the darkness is your friend

—*Bruce Cockburn*

CONTENTS

INTRODUCTION

The finder is an investigator, a musician and a poet, bringing the rhythm of music to poetry's form, and finding an unlikely partnership between the arts and the world of the detective.

The author is recounting with realism and humor, the mundane and the adventurous; surveillance in a dangerous inner city alley in Los Angeles, meetings with a witness in the bayous of Baton Rouge, searching for one-armed truck drivers in Detroit, or finding the bodies to match misplaced gravestones. Her journey is accompanied by the delicate interpretive drawings of noted German painter Hans Diebschlag, her friend of 30 years.

In these verses the author may someday find her mother's lost diamond ring, and the gun she though had been thrown into the dragon lake after a murder in her hometown. Mysteries have a way of solving, when you keep looking.

These are the musings of a lone female detective. She travels strange worlds that range between frightening and romantic. Under the radar, she reveals the terse adrenalized world of finding people, documents, motives, grails. And through her steady binoculars even catches some dazzling glimpses of her own soul.

—Nancy Wilson
(Heart)

PROLOGUE — WHAT'S IT LIKE?

People have always asked me what I do as a P.I. Is it like Magnum? I don't know how to answer.

It's an all-night surveillance in the snow in Connecticut, in a car with people you don't trust. Being chased by dogs in the slums of a California town, or being lost in a pitch-dark night, off road in the high desert, trying to find someone.

It's having an off duty policeman watch your back, when you're undercover doing a counterfeit software buy. It's having your cop boyfriend tell you he wouldn't do what you're doing or go where you are going, without a shotgun, a dog, and backup.

It's crying from the stories of cancer victims suffering from toxic exposure, or packing fear and steel to a deserted warehouse meeting with a stranger, in downtown L.A. And getting people to tell you about things they haven't told anyone.

It's tracking down corporate thieves on miles of paper, or finding homeless witnesses who saw all the chemical dumping and will swear to it in court. Having your witness scared off by wise guys, or investigating a suicide that is so sad you can barely stand it.

It's about trying to do a surveillance in Koreatown with four cars and radios and having to stop at red lights, or interviewing scientists to learn more than you ever wanted to know about rocket fuel, and how it got into the water.

It's saving your corporate client seventeen million dollars and not getting a percentage, or finding someone's brother who they had not seen in twenty-five years.

Tenacity and obsession. Your worst personal traits are your most useful professional ones. Ultimately it is about digging and compassion, and getting people to talk to you, without a badge.

THE FINDER

Poems of a Private Investigator

THE FINDER

Whatever was lost, I was
assigned to find it.
It didn't matter that I was ten.
That was always my job.

Many things I could find, but
I searched for years for my
mother's diamond ring, which
had fallen into the lake beside our home.
I never found it,
but I kept looking.

There was the murder.
Several streets over a man was shot
in his garage,
a suspected mafia hit.
Gun not found.

Later that same night,
a stranger was seen driving down
the Island Road,
out to the deserted peninsula.

I knew it was the perpetrator,
throwing his weapon into the lake.
I searched for the gun,
in the shallows off the island for years,
until I left home.

It must still be there,
rusting to pieces.

THE BOLD ONE

These bends in the road
exhaust the finite strength
of one's breath,
sap the texture from hair
that is pushed back off the
forehead a thousand times,
on the street,
in some noisy room,
on a hillside,
near the lake,
when down low behind the
freeway wheel,
doing this solo thing.

I have these meetings
between people,
in air conditioned rooms,
along satellite lines,
by video,
on the top of buildings,
in Spanish style bungalows,
standing on damp tile,
in dark theaters,
on a bench by a river,
over bed,
over gun barrel.

Love is love,

I have it
but I'm not holding anyone.
I'm reaching for clarity,
steadfast personal ground.
An hour after every dawn
I'm not even or certain.
At my desk I lose patience
for hard courage.
But at night
this boldness comes to me
which I store in small packets
behind certain words,
which I will use again
in solitude,
jostled on a sidewalk
or pushing hair out of my eyes
behind some wheel
blazing down the
human highway.

PERFECTLY CLEAN-FLIPSIDE

PERFECTLY CLEAN

I'm always looking for something
in this town. People, documents,
love.
Individuals are elusive, paper
becoming elusive.

There have been fruitless
endeavors.
Going from one seedy motel
to another,
with a photo of the deceased,
trying to find out where he
last stayed, just
before he stopped his own heart.

Or trying to find a guy in
South L.A. on a drug-barricaded
street.
Do Not Enter, unless you live here.
His mother answered the door holding
a sick baby. She was a heroin addict
if I ever saw one.
"I have a letter from his
brother, I'll give you the address,"
she said.
Both brothers were in the same jail.

This urban microcosm is not

always dark. When it's
not crushing,
it's diverse, teeming, amusing.
Instructive.

I was in the wholesale district downtown,
working a case of counterfeit goods.
We confirmed the target undercover,
then came in with
a U.S. Marshall, to
find not half a dozen as expected,
but truckloads of perfect Asian
reproductions.

I sat in my perfectly clean
Acura Legend in the alleyway,
watching the back door of the
warehouse with a video camera,
while the Marshall went in the front.
Don't chase if someone
runs, just shoot,
I was told.

I was not alone. The alley
was bustling with drug
commerce,
and a cardboard village.
The dealers ignored or laughed
at me, knowing they were not my
interest.

Everything went according to plan until I
saw flames in my rearview mirror
right behind the car.
Turned out a cardboard
city resident was
cooking a hotdog
in the gutter.
Burning part of his house.
Surveillance terminated.

DECLASSIFIED

Faces come to me, like so many flashes of memory.
Witnesses to some piece of history I needed to
investigate.
The lives I've reached into and drawn out,
pushed and prodded for their memory,
finessed and protected.

Conflict and pain mingled with pride.
The Manhattan Project scientist,
the weapons builder, the chemical chef,
the cipher technician,
the warrior.

I've read their diaries,
found their letters from Washington,
walked their bunkers,
seen their ships.

I found the military plan for San Diego,
June 1943.
In the event of an imminent hostile invasion,
orders were to destroy the Navy base,
blow up the piers, scuttle or set
fire to our ships in harbor.

Amidst this emergency, this fear,
they had to go to work every day
figure out how to raise a family,

get the laundry done,
buy cigarettes.

This was my father's generation,
and his father's.
They were stalked by war.
We are likewise haunted
foot soldiers,
but in a strange world, where everyone's
war comes to our media doorstep in
digital form.

There are still boot prints in the sand,
spent shells on the grieving ground,
somewhere.

DRAGON

I've come this far for the harvest moon.
It's full and ominous,
startling,
as it rears from this eastern horizon.

I'm part of the earth here,
the flaming October trees,
the granite that's scattered everywhere,
gray stones and gravestones.

I cut my strings accordingly,
when I heard the sirens speak.
I set off to another ocean,
and disappeared into myself.

The lake dragon that surrounded me
in this place as a child,
was at once benevolent and sinister,
equal parts fear and mystery.

The dragon still lives off the Island Road,
and carries the same deep attraction.
But now I can and will
walk away,
at first light.

POSSIBILITY FACTORS

The vast interior space of atoms
finds the nucleus nearly unseen,
unknown,
connected by probabilities.

Our environment is measured
by imperceptible particles
that touch and move within us,
without us.

In the physical world
I am part of the sky, the horizon,
part of the individual
standing near me.

The unlimited sea separating us
is minute,
The expanse of time is
imaginary.
We're surrounded by beings who
side step one another
in a continuous undiscernible dance,
like parts of atoms;
Invisible spirits who want to recognize
each other in a fixed place,
to know each other by pattern,
find something on which to hold.

Life is not defined by its repetitions
but by single extraordinary acts,
such as your life
such as mine.

DEAD ZONE

"Find out where the bodies are."
Five bodies,
to be specific.
I was given twenty-four hours.

I knew where the bodies were not.
They were not in the toxic dumpsite
where their gravestones
were found.
No bones, no caskets, not that the
bulldozers had found yet anyway.
 Just gravestones,
and a deadline.

First they found two.
Then three more.
I knew about this troublesome
real estate,
which is why I got called.
Tracking when, what,
and by whom it came into being,
so the EPA could figure out
who had to pay to fix it.

The engineers cleaning it up
had to report what they found,
within a day.
If there were no answers,

long-awaited remediation
would grind to a stiff halt.
A long investigation.
A bureaucratic nightmare.

I was sent photographs.
Intact old stones, mostly legible.
Names and dates.
None of the deceased were new to
this.
Dates of death were 1920's, 1940's.
Strangely spread out in time.
for a dumpsite that had been
shuttered for years.

I headed to the county
death records.
Not the ones where you get
neatly listed alphabetically,
by year, on microfiche.
The ones written in quill pen,
in large musty books with
broken bindings.

A lot of people died in childbirth
in 1920,
mothers and babies.
Fatalities from fires,
consumption,
death by gunshot.

Not so much cancer and heart disease.
Something else got you first.

Matching names, unmatched dates.
Right dates, wrong names.
Right names, right dates.
Walked out with death certificates
in hand.
Two were reported to be neighbors in
the same graveyard, three were not.
The graveyards were in different
towns, still no common thread.

I talked to caretakers,
went through card files
of inhabitants.
Walked the grounds
with a camera.
Documented the evidence.
Everyone was where they
were supposed to be.
Correctly placed, with a headstone.

Monument companies are supposed to
break up discarded stones.
not sell them off for someone
to build a patio,
like someone did recently
in the news.
Or toss them intact

in the local dump, for
someone to find thirty years later.

These people had good reason
to have their stones re-cut.
Most of them had family members
added later to their memorial.
One of them had their name
spelled wrong.
A final insult, corrected.

The one that nearly eluded me
died early, unmarried.
In the old mortuary cards
and the county records,
she was listed under a different last name.
But added to the family stone, eventually.
Found.

HAPPY HOUR

In the early morning,
the grey moist light
seeps like slow wine
into the room.

In a thousand places
someone is tasting
the same sunrise,
waking at the same latitude,
incredulous at the prospect
of another full cycle.

Before even rising I'm assessing
my commitment
to stand and walk and reason
and speak.

The subconscious, brain and spine
struggle for common ground.
There is no agreement from all parts
before reality subverts
the process.

So the feet hit the floor
without consensus,
and I am searching for balance
until sundown.

UNEQUIVOCAL

Soft Japanese music
in a dark hall
above a sphere of hard lights,
streets hushed,
but not without combustion
too far away to sense.

The pinpoints of heat
visually diminishing
two furlongs to the
close horizon
and the sea.

The dusk becoming the subsurface,
small cells of life,
vibrating torpidly between
this hill and the dream state,
being and becoming.

My love is absent or
distant,
with the taut plucked strings
muffled now,
indistinct.

Where will my voice be
if it seeks the surface again
from some nucleus

in the hidden earth
under these points of glass.

I must be motionless and
know the space within spaces,
like the Japanese rock garden,
quiet until the quiet
transforms.

SAN MIGUEL DE ALLENDE

The tequilas are stinging
in the San Miguel sun.
It is not the spoken words that matter,
but the quarter hour bell chimes,
and the stillness.

In the thin film of sweat,
misgivings drift,
dissolving their
grasp on my throat,
relinquishing the intensity that
I brought with me,
into the slow heat.

These guitar strings vibrate off the
ivy and rock cloister
that isolate me from humanity.
I wander among some notes
coming to me through the light,
until the quiet overwhelms.

Is there somewhere we can hear your song,
someone asks.
Yes, nightly,
room 215.

INTERNAL FORCES

Stark awake and invisible
at five A.M.,
porous with the freeway drone
three streets over,
permeating my body like distant machinery
intent on mastering my being.
Against this canvas I'm rushing
to locate a course
so as not to be defined by
external forces, but
by internal demand.

Like the crickets who mingle their
conversation with the street noise
in the dense air,
I'm displaced in the urban sprawl,
grieving sometimes for tall grass.

But I'm not alone on this desert coast.
I have found ports of reason
in an unreasoned landscape.
Against all preconception
there is something here to give.
Something.

SEVENTY-NINE BAYOU MILES

It's baking hot and the rain
just won't break.
The river is as still as it gets,
lapping at the concrete city,
immune to change.
The smell of the quay and the water
turns me inside out,
slow and hard.

I go to see some guy in Baton Rouge,
79 bayou miles from here.
A Mardi Gras chieftain,
who gives me beads and information.
I'll never see him again,
and I'm sorry.

I'm back down in the Big Easy,
sweating at the sounds and textures
that pull me out of my white skin.
These riverways course through my mind
like a drug,
and I can hardly stand
to leave.

DEBRIS FIELD

There is always a toxic waste pit near
your own hometown.
Casting a long shadow,
the product of human activity,
the debris field of urban life.

In this case it was on the Connecticut
border,
nearly hidden in the thick trees
off a dirt road.
Collecting the deleterious litter of
the Northeast, out of town
and sight.

I had to find the men who knew
the archeology,
filled out the trip logs,
saw the writing on the sides
of trucks,
because no one will take responsibility
unless it's shoved in their
corporate face.

It's cradle to grave, doesn't matter
if it was 1950.
Find the witness, find the
proof, and they
will be made to pay, to turn

the dirt into
something less ominous.

There is a mythology about every site,
central figures emerge.
Find that guy. He knows everything.
I tracked him to a house in a small town.
Peeling paint and crooked stairs, a haunted
three stories and no answer at the door.

Wait and wait some more, everyone
comes home eventually.
He was not surprised to see me,
just like the movies, they expect one day
someone will show up and want to know
what they saw.

A grizzled man, shock grey hair under his cap,
animated, seventy-five.
Hours in his haunted old house
at the dining table,
smoke reeking from the curtains.
Not wanting a glass of water from
the dubious kitchen sink,
but taking everything else he offered.

His brother also worked there, their
cousin hauled in waste solvents.
A guy from high school dumped the oil
of every machine shop in town.

The utility brought PCBs,
the sticky mud was
bulldozed into layers,
watered with Hartford's industrial soup,
drained to the river.

He wasn't afraid. This was good.
People stop worrying
about retribution on the way to eighty.
He chain smoked and coughed
while he spilled names and
years and truckloads.
I came back two days later
with a notary public
and an attorney.

He coughed out smoke and information,
and possibly more.
Six months later I tested positive
for latent tuberculosis,
spent the better part of a year
taking pills
to knock it down.

He's probably still kicking,
basking in the power
a nobody can have
against the
toxic corporate beast,
when holding the cards.

THE GENUINE ARTICLE

There is a swarm of tartan humanity
along the Royal Edinburgh Mile,
by the pint,
by the half pint,
on the hills over Holyrood,
looking east to the Firth of Forth,
inhaling the North Sea air,
the closes and smell of grain,
sliding down the green way.

It always comes to me here,
Edinburgh, my spiritual zone.
Pipes and affirmation
lost and found.
Urban and ancient,
my pilgrimage,
urban and ancient.

SEARCH

Somewhere in this mottled landscape
viewed from 30,000 feet,
below the cotton fragments of air,
there is a collective inland harbor of souls.

I don't know who these people are,
but I keep looking for them,
a finder at heart,
a bloodhound off leash.

On the convoluted discovery trail,
I am distracted by the rock canyons,
the desert and the sea.

I get mixed up in needs and challenge,
waylaid by the sparkle and soft,
in the search for commonality
with others,
proof of life.

MISSING PARTS

You could never have guessed how many
one-armed truck drivers there were
in Detroit until you
went looking for one.

Sometimes that's all I've had to go on.
One arm, or even one leg, or a name
like "Shorty."
The revolving door of waste haulers
who have been party
to a toxic waste investigation,
had a plethora of missing parts.

Detroit seemed to have more that its
share of one-armed truck drivers,
men with only a nickname,
and contaminated landfills.
There was also a lot of mafia.

I spent one fine summer afternoon
talking to one of the latter. Not to
ask him about his experiences or
his business partners,
which would have been foolish.

But he was more than happy to
share information about people
who were not his family, so to speak.

He wore lizard skin cowboy boots,
and a large gold chain.
He was missing his trigger finger.

The colleague who I was with
was worried about that fellow.
I thought he was kind of nice.
What was not nice, was
looking for the driver
who was short one appendage,
in the projects of Detroit.

The rough streets
in my own city,
do not make me half as nervous
as those of another town.
Knocking on doors on the
back side of Detroit,
did not make me popular.

But there was no other way. These
guys were not in an online database.
You found them at home, or in the local bar.
Otherwise they were on the road,
they were dead
or they were just missing.

The other investigator on the case
who looked under a sensitive rock,
had his life threatened.

Our best witness was compromised.
The case fell apart, nearly.

And like almost every toxic waste
case I've ever worked,
you learned about things you
did not want to hear about,
when you started asking questions.

There were drivers hauling junk chemicals
that didn't even make it to the landfill.
You could empty a tanker truck on the
highway between Detroit and Chicago
on the five hour drive,
by opening the spigot
just a little.
More things went missing.

SEVEN SISTERS
(HANS)

The Seven Sisters haven't changed,
bearing chalk white horses and
sheer cliffs.
In seven and ten years since walking these
stone beaches last,
not even my heart is much different.
It must take more Celtic ages
than this to erode land or soul.

Perhaps time hasn't much passed,
and I've only stepped away long enough
to change clothes,
and slip pixels into my camera.

My love for you is the same constant,
and we still laugh at ourselves.
Your hands still draw the minute colors
of your dreams.
Mine, mysteries and harmonies.

The only obvious measure of change
is the boy who is not
in today's photograph,
because he's already in his own image.
He is a strapping good looker version of that
little one who used to knock about
your side.

We still look for balance in
the cross hairs of light
framing the trees,
the cliffs and the ghosts of
Britain.

That's why I still come here.
For the sake of balance,
and for you my darling friend.

HE WAS HER SON

There are parts of South Central Los Angeles
that can be very lonely,
when you don't know where
you are going.

Pockets of young men in sleeveless
T-shirts watched me as I drove slowly by.
They were sweating in the deep dusk,
perched on porches and draped around
hot street corners,
drinking and smoking.

I drove up and down the street,
haltingly,
in the wrong kind of car,
looking for an address that
I had to find, a witness to a wrongful
death case.

I meant to get there before dark,
but lost the sun.
Young and white,
an anomaly
in this urban discontent.
Looking misplaced or maybe
searching for drugs, but
stupid, in either case.

I couldn't find the address.
It was just not where it was
supposed to be.
Anxiety turned inward.
Murmurings and catcalls.
Like the streets of Amsterdam,
though that vibe was sexual,
this was sarcastic with a dash of sinister.

No one moved toward me.
This was my city, therefore my barrios.
Armed only with arrogance,
I wasn't stupid enough to carry
a gun in this hood.
There were enough guns already.

This place was teeming with frustration,
the danger of getting caught
in someone else's cross fire,
someone else's dispute,
of which there were many here.

I wandered down a couple of
driveways, between some
ramshackle single family digs in need of
nails and paint.
Found what should be, numerically speaking,
the right place – it was in the back,
behind another house.
A small cottage with broken steps.

I banged on the screen door.
A short, thin, mulatto woman in her 50s
appeared, looking at me over big glasses that
were halfway down her nose.
I told her the name of the man I was seeking,
a witness to a suspicious death
where he had worked in a nursing home.
The lawyers had lost track of him before trial.

He was her son. But he wasn't home.
She opened the door, not in the least afraid.
She took my card to have him call me.
"How did you find us?" she asked.
"It wasn't easy," I said.
"God helped you," she said, "and
God protected you."

SPECTATORS

They're sitting,
they're watching,
they're standing,
alone or together
or back up against the jetty wall.

They're having that last sweet cigarette,
or pouring their hearts out.

We're all looking seaward,
silhouetted against the
oceanscape,
the musky turquoise Pacific.

The evening is transforming
cirrus clouds into streaks
of red desire.
Malibu is subtle in the distance,
and steel birds pace their lazy way
overhead in a fragmented design.

I'm the slide on the strings
playing into my ears,
the wheels of this fast bike machine
and part of the scenery.

Nowhere in life have I
felt so strongly

the thoughts of others, the
scattered beings on this beach,
perfectly still,
or pacing slowly
at the ends of land.

We are all the common thread,
that ties us.

EXPECTATIONS

I love that people fly in and out
of my town like
doves on the wing.

I love that I can see a blue heron
crouching in the wetlands,
thinking he's invisible.

I love that you get what you
pay for,
when you buy a Mercedes.

And that even when you get nothing,
you still have what you give.

BACKLOT

The soft shades of afternoon light spear
the streets,
and jut through the iron staircases
of the buildings in this false city.
Like a quiet watcher,
I am on the border.

Amidst this visionary tangle
of back lot sets,
I keep to my own choice of legends,
avoid the entrapments,
keep to my own.

TIME OUT

I have nightmares
breaking my sleep,
scattering dreams like dust.
Old anxieties,
drawing on the unsettled score,
time owed and
abandoned.

I have courted emptiness
as well as gain.
Still, in the vacuum of
dark and
the absence of sky,
I have missed you,
coming and leaving.

PACKING

These fractions of time
bend and surprise,
find me willing or coerced
by fortune.

Today I'm light and thankful,
going 85 on the 101 South
with the fog slipping in
along the Ventura County line.

I've been here in this
germination stage before,
trying to find a strength
where there was none.
Now I'm packed and ready,
in the passing lane.

LOTHIAN STREET

Shadows stretch across the room
from the window of muffled highway,
to the stream of metal light beside me.
Nineteen nineties blue light,
indifferent heat.

In the slice of midnight,
I remember a cleared foot trail
edged by wild flowers,
leading to a high meadow
above the old town.
On the hillside
you held me and
someone took our picture.
I don't even remember
someone else being there.

But someone was always there
In a small flat near Holyrood Palace,
crowded,
until you stepped past
the bedding, into the garden.

My hair was long and my hand
spread against your chest,
keeping your heart inside.
I dreamt for years
of finding you.

But you moved to the Highlands
and married the woman who was
in the garden.
You're probably commuting now
from crag to oil rig,
or moor to midlands.
Supporting two children
and Christine.

I'm living in Los Angeles
following my heart in circles.
You would barely know me,
except I still write poems
by torchlight.

HUMAN CONDITION

I released my Grandmother's butterflies today,
that had been pressed in a locket
for ten decades.
Set free on a hillside
in the high grass by the lake
under the Hollywood sign.

They were added to the wind
along the Mulholland skyline
to join the many souls that muster there
at dusk,
to measure us by our grace,
our emotion,
our originality and composition.

We left over souls,
languid in our human condition,
are judged by how we
stack up against the gods
and the muses.

They watch us watching the clock,
knowing
unlike us,
when it's time.

CAT CANYON

I am navigating this ribbon of road
between cities,
along the edge of Cat Canyon
and the continent.

The long bullet searchlight,
flaring off steel beams and concrete walls.
I can't hide in this tunnel,
from what happened to you.

I've got your smell
on my face and hands.
I waited for you
in a dark car,
I couldn't leave you behind.

I can't hide from the shreds of sound,
the prism of shattered fragments
strewn along the coastal highway.

I waited for you
in a dark car.
I can't leave you behind.

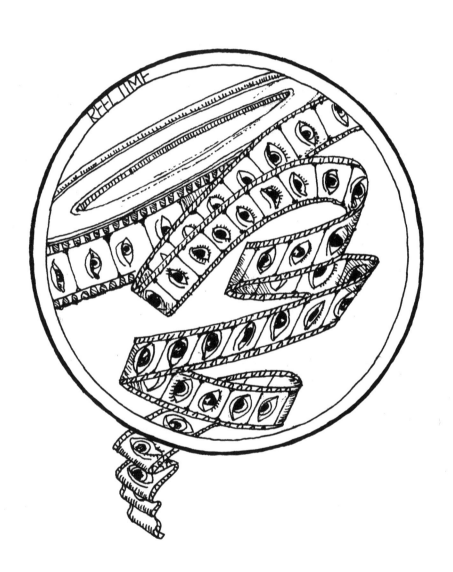

REEL TIME

Outside time,
fiction is the preferred medium,
but fantasy is a dreamstate in
sleep only.
Reality burns like daylight.

Mind picture,
blink.
Blurred vision,
blink.
Road not travelled,
blink.
Nighttime eyes open,
blink.
Open road ahead,
blink.

LIGHT

This coat of tears you are shedding,
the cloak of past commitments and hopes,
of dual strife and striving,
needs not met,
is a burden no one should have to carry.

You have taken the highest road,
reached until your arms were wide open,
put your heart in danger
and still asked again,
if you could be found worthy.

It is not the right question.
You are not the vacuum.
Love doesn't stop at your door,
it pervades your house like incense,
touches those you know like grace.

This shadow that is crossing you
will bleach out against the light.

MARSHLAND

These songs speak to me
like the rustle of quail
against reed,
in a vast marshland,
dense at six am,
stillness barely touched.

In real time I am
on an asphalt river
moving at a fast walk
against the current of cars.

Inside my marshlands
I am toeing the catwalk
which is creaking underfoot,
sinking into wetlands
where the boards have weathered.

I'm watching through binoculars
for motion or wing,
listening to the crickets
against my memory,
Careful, least the sidewalk
disappear.

ROOTS MUSIC

How come you know so much about love?
This profound, visceral music at the root
of all movement,
all motion.
Maybe you were at the center
of some cosmic coincidence that
kept your heart open and
allowed you to dream.

I haven't been so touched by family
since I found my first kindred
souls in the grooves of long playing records
a lifetime ago,
a childhood ago.

If I hadn't lived this long,
I would have missed this last
fast and straight train ride
with dreamers like myself.

Look at pretty windows
At shiny people
Statues under sparking lights

Just take a picture
A melting moment
Flashing on this crazy ride

Just close your eyes now
And breath a sigh now
We're getting out of here
Out of here

Riding the wheels
Riding the wheels

—Heart

A NOTE ABOUT THE ILLUSTRATOR

Hans Diebschlag is a painter who works mainly with oils and oil/tempera mixes using traditional glazing or overlay techniques. He paints figurative pictures often with a strong narrative content that are rich in symbolism and detail.

Hans's paintings often reflect his interest in the spiritual with juxtapositions of eastern and western themes. Another major theme relates to Rüsselsheim, the German town where Hans grew up and which is home to the car manufacturer Opel. Although Hans has lived in England for more than 30 years he retains strong connections to Rüsselsheim and Opel.

Diebschlag's work has been exhibited internationally since 1982 and his paintings are in private, corporate and municipal collections worldwide. A gallery of his work may be viewed at www.diebschlag.com.

A NOTE ABOUT THE AUTHOR

Julie Bergman lived and worked in Boston and Cambridge until emigrating to Los Angeles, where she became involved in the music business, wrote feature articles for magazines, and traveled regularly to the British Isles. She began her career as a licensed detective in 1987. She continues to live in California and work as a Private Investigator, with a specialty in environmental investigations. Her first book of poetry is titled "Los Angeles Fires of the Heart." www.juliebergman.com